LaKisha Monique Swift

IF AI AND I WERE PRESIDENT:

A ROADMAP FOR LEADERSHIP IN THE 21ST CENTURY

INTRODUCTION: SETTING THE STAGE FOR A SMARTER FUTURE

Did You Know the U.S. Government Wastes Over $2 Trillion Every Year?

Yep. You read that right. According to multiple reports, **government inefficiency, wasteful spending, and outdated systems** cost taxpayers **trillions** — every single year. Meanwhile, working-class people are out here trying to figure out how to afford groceries while CEOs get tax breaks big enough to buy their third yacht.

Now, I don't know about you, but I have a serious problem with that.

Hi, I'm Lakisha, and I've spent a lot of time watching how **power, money, and leadership** work in this country — and let me tell you, we can do better. Actually, we *have* to do better.

I've worked in **corporate, entertainment, business, and even caregiving** — and I've seen firsthand how **bad policies, corporate greed, and government inaction** impact everyday people. I've seen billion-dollar companies waste money like it's Monopoly cash while the average worker can't even get a decent raise. I've seen renters struggle while corporations buy up entire neighborhoods just to jack up prices. And I've seen politicians argue about problems they have no intention of solving—because **fixing things doesn't make them money.**

That's why I started thinking: **What if leadership actually worked? What if we used common sense, technology, and real-world solutions instead of outdated political nonsense?**

That's where AI comes in.

No, I'm not saying we should hand over the White House to a robot (*though, let's be honest, it might handle things better than some past leaders*). What I *am* saying is that **the way we lead, solve problems, and make decisions has to evolve—just like everything else in the 21st century.**

This book isn't about replacing human leadership with AI. It's about **using AI as a tool to help us lead smarter, faster, and fairer.** Imagine a world where:
✅ **Healthcare costs go down because AI eliminates waste and price gouging.** ✅ **Government programs actually work because they're based on real-time data, not guesswork.** ✅ **We invest in innovation and job creation instead of outdated systems that hold us back.** ✅ **We tax fairly, spend wisely, and stop rewarding corporations for bad behavior.**

Sounds good, right? Well, that's exactly what this book is about—**a roadmap for leadership that makes sense.**

Why This Book? Why Now?

We're living in an era where **technology is advancing at breakneck speed** —but government is still stuck in the past. While the private sector is out here developing AI that can write poetry and self-driving cars that (mostly) don't crash, our leaders are still arguing over things like **whether climate change is real and if billionaires should pay taxes.**

It's time to change that.

This book is for **everyone who's tired of broken systems**—for the people who believe that **we can have a thriving economy, fair governance, and a future that actually works for all of us.**

Whether you're a **frustrated voter, a business owner, a policymaker, or just someone who wants to know how AI could make leadership better**, this book is for you.

So let's dive in—because if AI and I were president, we'd actually get some things done.

📖 Dedication

This book is dedicated to **my Mommy, Charmaine and my brother Charlie.**

To my **Mommy**, my biggest cheerleader—your strength, love, and resilience have shaped me into the person I am today. You taught me how to stand tall, fight for what's right, and believe in my own power. **This book is as much yours as it is mine.**

To my **brother Charlie**, my forever protector and partner-in-crime—you've been with me through every twist and turn. No matter what life threw at us, we had each other. **This book is proof that we rise, we thrive, and we keep pushing forward.**

I love you both more than words can ever express.

TABLE OF CONTENTS

📖 CHAPTER 1: WHY GOVERNMENT IS BROKEN (AND HOW WE FIX IT)

Let's be honest—if you want to understand why **nothing ever gets done in Washington**, look no further than the broken systems that are running the show. **The bureaucracy, the corporate influence, the outdated policies**— it's like the government is stuck in a bad episode of a reality TV show, where the rules keep changing and nobody knows what's going on.

Here's the deal: The **problem is not the people**, it's the **system**.

For decades, **politicians have fought for their own re-election rather than long-term solutions**. Why? Because when you're **funded by lobbyists** who want to keep the status quo, it's a lot easier to say, "Let's just do what's comfortable" rather than push for real change. And let's not forget about the **bureaucracy**—it's like a giant paper mill that churns out more paperwork than it does solutions. You know those forms you have to fill out every time you apply for a government benefit? Imagine that on a national scale, with **endless red tape** and policies that change more than the weather.

But here's where **AI** comes in.

AI doesn't care about **party lines** or **special interests**. It just looks at the data, analyzes it, and says, "Here's what's working, here's what isn't." Imagine using AI to look at our **entire system**, and instantly recommend the most efficient, cost-effective, and fair policies. Forget the 500-page bills that nobody reads—AI could help lawmakers **cut through the noise** and get straight to the solutions that actually **work**.

In the next chapters, we'll dive into how AI can help us tackle some of the biggest problems we face:

- **Economic inequality**
- **Healthcare costs**
- **Government waste**
- **Job creation and automation**

But first, let's take a look at why **government inefficiency** is so deeply ingrained—and how we can finally fix it.

📖 CHAPTER 2: A BALANCED ECONOMY – THRIVING CAPITALISM WITH FAIR PLAY

Let's talk about **money**.

We've all heard the phrase **"If you work hard, you'll succeed."** Sounds great, right? Very **American Dream, very motivational poster with a bald eagle flying over a**

mountain. But let's be real—**that's not how the economy actually works for most people.**

For decades, the system has been **rigged to benefit the wealthy** while everyday people keep hustling just to survive. **Wages have barely budged in 40 years** while the cost of living has skyrocketed. Meanwhile, billionaires are out here **hoarding wealth like it's a high-score competition**, and corporations are getting tax breaks for moving jobs overseas.

And then there's **trickle-down economics**, the biggest scam ever sold to the American people. We were told that **if we cut taxes for the rich, the benefits would "trickle down" to the rest of us.** Spoiler alert: They didn't. Instead of reinvesting in American workers, **corporations pocketed the profits,**

shipped jobs overseas, and bought back their own stock to make themselves richer.

So what's the fix? We don't punish success—we **reward businesses that actually reinvest in America. We stop incentivizing greed** and start rewarding companies that create **jobs, pay fair wages, and strengthen communities.**

🚀 Step 1: Corporate Tax Reform – The "Do Good, Pay Less" Rule

Right now, **big corporations are getting away with murder** when it comes to taxes. Some of the richest companies in the world—**Amazon, Tesla, Google**—have paid **little to no federal income tax** in certain years, despite making **billions** in profit. How? **Loopholes, offshore tax havens, and a system that rewards greed.**

That ends under our plan.

🔷 **The New Rule:**

- If a company **creates jobs in the U.S., pays fair wages, and invests in American infrastructure** → **they get tax breaks**.
- If a company **outsources jobs, underpays workers, or avoids taxes by stashing money overseas** → **they pay up, no exceptions.**
- No more **corporate welfare** for billion-dollar companies who don't contribute to the economy.

We don't tax success—we tax exploitation.

🏥 Step 2: Healthcare That Doesn't Bankrupt You

Did you know that the **#1 cause of bankruptcy in the U.S. is medical debt?** In **every other developed nation**, healthcare is a **basic right**, not a **luxury only the rich can afford**.

🔷 **Our Plan:**

✅ **Negotiate Drug Prices – Other countries do it, so why are Americans paying 10x more for the same meds?**

✅ **Expand the Public Option – If private insurance works for you, great. But everyone should have access to** affordable healthcare.

✅ **Eliminate Medical Debt Predation** – Hospitals shouldn't be suing low-income patients for thousands of dollars while they rake in billions in revenue.

Healthcare **shouldn't be a business model—it should be a basic human right.**

🏠 Step 3: Housing Reform – Homes Over Hedge Funds

Ever wonder why **rent keeps going up, but wages don't?** It's not an accident—it's a **rigged system** where corporations and hedge funds buy up homes, **artificially drive up prices**, and then turn around and rent them at outrageous rates.

🔷 The Fix:

✅ **Ban Corporate Home Hoarding** – If a hedge fund owns **thousands of homes** but refuses to sell or rent them, they get hit with a **progressive vacancy tax**. No more gaming the market.

✅ **Affordable Housing Investment** – We **incentivize developers** to build more affordable homes through **public-**

private partnerships.

✅ **End Discriminatory Lending** – Black and Brown communities have been **systematically denied mortgages and loans** for decades. We create **AI-powered oversight** to track and **eliminate discriminatory banking practices**.

A home should be **something you live in, not a financial game for Wall Street.**

💰 Step 4: Closing the Racial Wealth Gap – Real Economic Equality

Let's talk about the **elephant in the room**: **The racial wealth gap didn't happen by accident.**

For centuries, Black, Latino, and Indigenous communities have been **systematically locked out** of wealth-building opportunities:

- **Redlining & Housing Discrimination** – Black families were **denied home loans** for decades, making it harder to build generational wealth.
- **Wage Gaps** – Studies show that **Black and Latino workers** make significantly **less** than white workers **for the same job.**

- **Predatory Lending & Higher Interest Rates** – Banks have a history of **charging minorities higher rates** on loans, mortgages, and credit.

🔷 **The Fix:**

✅ **Equal Pay Enforcement** – We use **AI-driven payroll analysis** to **expose and eliminate racial pay gaps** in real time.

✅ **First-Time Minority Homebuyer Incentives** – We **increase access to home loans** for Black, Latino, and Indigenous families.

✅ **Support for Minority-Owned Businesses** – We **expand**

federal grants and **cut red tape** for minority entrepreneurs, making it easier to build businesses.

Economic **fairness isn't just a talking point—it's a necessity.**

🔄 **Recap: The Future of Capitalism Is Fair Play**

📌 **We don't punish success—we reward ethical business.**

📌 **Healthcare should be affordable, not a financial death sentence.**

📌 **Housing should be for people, not hedge funds.**

📌 **Equal pay and wealth-building opportunities for all, not just the privileged few.**

This is how we create a thriving economy that works for everyone.

📖 CHAPTER 3: THE ROLE OF AI IN MODERN GOVERNANCE

Government, But Make It Smart

Let's be honest—**government isn't exactly known for efficiency.**

We've all seen it:

- A new law gets proposed, and suddenly, **it takes years** to pass because politicians are arguing about nonsense.
- Government programs meant to **help people** are so **complicated and outdated** that **no one can figure out how to use them.**
- Meanwhile, corporations are **running circles around regulators** because government agencies are using **technology from 1995** to track problems happening in 2025.

Here's the thing: **If Amazon can predict what kind of toothpaste you need before you do, the U.S. government should be able to process a tax refund faster than three months.**

This is where **AI comes in**.

🤖 Step 1: AI as the Ultimate Fact-Checker

Politicians love to bend the truth, exaggerate, or just flat-out lie. They know that by the time fact-checkers expose them, people have already moved on to the next headline.

🔷 **How AI Fixes This:**

✅ **Instant Fact-Checking** – AI could **scan political speeches, debates, and campaign ads in real time**, flagging **misinformation as it happens.**

✅ **Transparent Policy Tracking** – Imagine a public AI system where you can **type in any law or policy** and immediately see **who benefits, who loses, and what the actual numbers are.**

✅ **No More "We Need More Studies" Excuses** – AI can **analyze years of data in seconds**, so politicians can't delay action by claiming they need **more research** on things we already know (*looking at you, climate change deniers*).

📊 **Step 2: AI for Smarter Budgets (No More $500 Hammers)**

Ever hear about the **$500 hammer?**

That's right—the Pentagon once paid **$500 for a single hammer** and **$640 for a toilet seat** because of bad accounting, corruption, and waste. And that's just a tiny drop in the ocean of **government inefficiency**.

🔷 How AI Fixes This:

✅ **Real-Time Budget Tracking** – AI can scan **government spending in real-time**, flagging **wasteful, duplicate, or fraudulent purchases** instantly.

✅ **Fraud Detection** – No more **corporate scammers overcharging** the government for simple goods and services. AI can **cross-check invoices** and **block shady contracts** before they happen.

✅ **Taxpayer Transparency** – Imagine an AI-driven dashboard where you can **see exactly where your tax dollars are going**—down to the last penny.

Government should be accountable to the people, not special interests. AI makes that possible.

⚖️ Step 3: AI for Equal Justice (Because the System is Broken)

Let's be real—**America's justice system is not "equal" for everyone.**

If you're rich and powerful, you can get away with a **slap on the wrist** for crimes that **send poor people to prison for decades**.

Black and Brown communities, in particular, face **harsher sentences, racial profiling, and wrongful convictions** at alarming rates.

🔷 **How AI Fixes This:**

✅ **Bias Detection in Sentencing** – AI can **analyze thousands of court cases** and **flag racial bias** in sentencing, ensuring **equal punishment for equal crimes**.

✅ **Police Body Cam Analysis** – AI can **review police footage** to detect **excessive force, racial profiling, or misconduct**, making accountability automatic.

✅ **Predicting & Preventing Wrongful Convictions** – AI can **cross-check forensic evidence, witness statements, and trial**

records, catching **mistakes before innocent people go to prison.**

AI **doesn't replace judges or police officers**—but it **keeps the system honest** by exposing discrimination and corruption.

🏛 **Step 4: AI for Elections (Because Democracy Shouldn't Be a Mess)**

The **U.S. voting system** is a **hot mess**.

- Every election, we see **voter suppression**, **misinformation**, and **glitches that "accidentally" favor one side over the other**.
- We have **outdated voting machines**, confusing ballots, and election processes that vary wildly **from state to state**.

- And don't even get me started on **gerrymandering**, where politicians **literally redraw maps to rig elections in their favor**.

🔷 **How AI Fixes This:**

✅ **AI-Driven Voter Registration** – No more sketchy purges of voter rolls. AI can **detect wrongful removals** and **ensure everyone eligible can vote**.

✅ **Fair Redistricting** – AI can **draw fair voting districts** based on **real population data**, eliminating gerrymandering.

✅ **Election Security** – AI can **detect voting irregularities** and **prevent election fraud**, ensuring a **secure and fair vote count**.

🚀 **AI + Human Leadership = A Government That Works**

Here's the bottom line: **AI won't replace human leadership—but it will make it smarter.**

📌 **Politicians won't be able to lie without getting instantly fact-checked.**

📌 **Taxpayers will know exactly where their money is going.**

📌 **Racial bias in the justice system can be detected and eliminated.**

📌 **Elections will be safer, fairer, and more transparent.**

Government should work for the people—not for corporations, special interests, or career politicians. AI is how we make that happen.

📖 CHAPTER 4: YEAR 1 – STABILIZATION & TRUST-BUILDING

Step One: Fix the Foundation Before We Build

If you've ever tried to fix a house with a **cracked foundation**, you know the truth: **it doesn't matter how nice your renovations are—if the base is broken, the whole thing will collapse.**

That's exactly where we are as a country.

- **People don't trust the government.** (For good reason.)
- **The economy is uneven.** (The rich get richer, while working people struggle.)
- **The justice system is broken.** (Ask anyone who isn't rich and white.)

So before we start making **big moves**, we **stabilize.**

📌 **We eliminate the biggest sources of government waste.**

📌 **We restore economic balance so working people can breathe.**

📌 **We put an end to corporate greed that exploits the system.**

📌 **We rebuild trust by making government work for real people—not just the wealthy elite.**

Here's how we **get it done in Year One.**

🏛 Step 1: Cut Government Waste Without Hurting People

There's a **huge difference** between **smart cuts** and **dumb cuts.**

Dumb cuts are what we usually get: Slashing **education, healthcare, and social programs**—you know, the things people actually need.

Smart cuts go after **government waste, fraud, and inefficiency**—the stuff that **sucks up tax dollars and gives nothing in return.**

🔷 How We Fix It:

✅ **AI-powered audits of every federal department** – No more bloated contracts, no more duplicate programs. **Every dollar gets tracked.**

✅ **Eliminate overpriced government contractors** – No more paying **$500 for hammers or $1,200 for office chairs**.

✅ **Cut congressional perks** – If you're in Congress, **you don't get lifetime benefits while voting against healthcare for regular people.**

The result? Billions in savings—without cutting what people actually need.

💰 Step 2: Economic Reset – "Level the Playing Field"

Right now, the **economic game is rigged**.

- **Corporations don't pay taxes.** (Meanwhile, workers see their paychecks shrink.)
- **Wages haven't kept up with inflation.** (Everything costs more, but you're not making more.)
- **Black and Brown communities have been systemically shut out of wealth-building.** (That stops now.)

🔷 **Our Year-One Economic Plan:**

✅ **Middle-Class Tax Relief** – If you make under $100K, **you see a tax cut.**

✅ **Corporate Responsibility Tax Plan** – Companies **only get tax breaks if they reinvest in America—no more rewards for outsourcing jobs.**

✅ **Fair Pay Act** – We use **AI-driven payroll audits** to **expose and eliminate racial and gender pay gaps.**

✅ **Small Business Stimulus** – If you run a small or minority-owned business, **you get federal support—because Wall Street has enough handouts.**

If you work hard, you should be able to build wealth. No exceptions.

🏥 Step 3: Healthcare That Actually Works for People

Nobody should go bankrupt because they got sick. Period.

The U.S. **spends more on healthcare than any other nation** — yet somehow, we still get **worse results**.

🔷 **How We Fix It in Year One:**

✅ **Negotiate Drug Prices Like Other Countries** – If Canada and Europe pay less, so should we.

✅ **Expand Public Option** – If you like your private insurance, keep it. But **if you don't, you should have an affordable alternative.**

✅ **End Medical Debt Predation** – Hospitals shouldn't be **suing poor patients** while making **billions in profit.**

Healthcare should be a right, not a privilege for the wealthy.

⚖️ Step 4: Criminal Justice Reform – No More Two-Tiered System

Let's be blunt: **The justice system isn't broken — it's working exactly as it was designed to.** And that's the problem.

- If you're rich, you get **fined**.
- If you're poor, you get **time.**

That **ends now.**

🔷 Our Year-One Criminal Justice Plan:

✅ **Eliminate Cash Bail for Nonviolent Offenses** – No more **sitting in jail for months just because you can't afford bail.**

✅ **End For-Profit Prisons** – Private prisons **make money by keeping people locked up.** That's not justice.

✅ **Police Accountability & Bias Tracking** – AI-powered **body cam analysis** keeps **officers accountable** for misconduct.

✅ **Legalize Marijuana & Expunge Records** – People shouldn't be in prison for something that's legal in half the country.

The law should work the same for everyone—no special treatment for the rich.

🗳️ Step 5: Restore Trust in Elections (Because Democracy Shouldn't Be This Messy)

Voter suppression, **rigged districts, misinformation, and endless debates about mail-in ballots**—it's **embarrassing** how outdated our election system is.

🔷 How We Fix It in Year One:

✅ **AI-Powered Election Security** – Stop hacking, fraud, and voter suppression in real-time.

✅ **Automatic Voter Registration** – If you turn 18, **you're automatically registered—no more hurdles.**

✅ **End Gerrymandering** – AI draws **fair districts based on real population data, not political bias. Fair elections shouldn't be a debate— they should be a guarantee.**

🔄 **Recap: What We Accomplish in Year One**

📌 **We cut waste without cutting essential services.**

📌 **We level the economic playing field.**

📌 **We fix healthcare to work for regular people.**

📌 **We make the justice system fair and accountable.**

📌 **We secure our elections and restore trust in democracy.**

This is how we build a government that actually works.

📖 CHAPTER 5: YEAR 2 – GROWTH & EXPANSION

We Fixed the Foundation—Now Let's Build

Now that **the economy isn't rigged, healthcare isn't bankrupting people, and elections aren't a mess**, it's time to **take America to the next level.**

- **We're rebuilding our infrastructure.**
- **We're creating future-proof jobs.**
- **We're expanding homeownership so people can actually afford to live.**

This isn't about temporary fixes—it's about setting up an economy that works for generations to come.

Here's how we make **Year 2 the year of opportunity and expansion.**

🚧 Step 1: Infrastructure & Jobs – "Build America 2.0"

The U.S. used to be the world leader in infrastructure. Now? We have **crumbling roads, outdated airports, and bridges held together by duct tape and prayers.** Meanwhile, other countries are **leaving us in the dust** with **high-speed rail, modern power grids, and clean energy systems.**

🔷 **Our Year 2 Infrastructure Plan:**

✅ **Massive Federal Investment in Roads, Bridges, and Clean Energy** – Millions of **high-paying jobs** created through **infrastructure projects.**

✅ **High-Speed Rail Expansion** – It's embarrassing that **Europe and Japan** have high-speed trains while **our best option is still the Greyhound bus.**

✅ **Water & Power Upgrades** – No more **Flint, Michigan situations.** Every city deserves **clean water, reliable electricity, and modernized grids.**

✅ **Public-Private Partnerships** – The government partners with **U.S. companies** to fund projects, ensuring **long-term economic growth.**

📌 **More jobs. Better infrastructure. A stronger economy.**

💡 Step 2: AI & Tech – The Future of Work, Not the End of Jobs

Let's address the **elephant in the room**: **AI and automation are replacing jobs.**

But here's the thing—**they don't have to.**

Every major technological revolution (electricity, the internet, automation) has wiped out some jobs—but it also created millions of new ones. The problem is **we aren't training workers fast enough for these new jobs.**

🔷 **How We Fix It:**

✅ **AI Job Retraining Programs** – If AI **eliminates your job, you get free training** for a **new, higher-paying job in tech, clean energy, or skilled trades.**

✅ **Automation Tax on Job Replacements** – If a company **replaces human workers with AI, they pay a tax that funds retraining programs.**

✅ **Tech Equity Fund for Black & Brown Communities** – Minority communities **have been shut out of tech for too long**—we create grants and scholarships to **increase access to high-paying tech careers.**

✅ **AI Oversight Board** – AI should **enhance jobs, not eliminate them**—a national AI board ensures **ethical AI development.**

📌 **Technology should work for us—not against us.**

🏠 Step 3: Housing Reform – Making Homes Affordable Again

Right now, **the housing market is a joke.**

- **Rents are skyrocketing.**
- **Wages aren't keeping up.**
- **Corporate landlords are buying up houses and jacking up prices.**

And **young people, working-class families, and communities of color are being priced out.**

🔷 **How We Fix It in Year 2:**

✅ **Corporate Housing Crackdown** – Hedge funds that **buy up homes and leave them empty** get hit with **a heavy tax until they sell or rent them at fair prices.**

✅ **National Rent Stabilization Act** – No more **insane rent hikes** that price people out of their homes.

✅ **Affordable Housing Expansion** – We **partner with developers** to build **high-quality, affordable housing**—because nobody should have to **work 3 jobs just to afford rent.**

✅ **Black & Latino Homeownership Grants** – We expand **access to home loans** for **historically excluded communities.**

📌 **Housing is a basic need, not a Wall Street game.**

🔋 Step 4: Energy Independence – Clean, Affordable, American-Made Energy

Let's be real: **The world is moving toward clean energy whether we like it or not.**

- **China owns the solar industry.**
- **Europe is miles ahead on green energy.**
- **Meanwhile, the U.S. is still debating if climate change is real.**

That stops in Year 2.

🔷 **Our Clean Energy Plan:**

✅ **Massive Investment in U.S.-Made Clean Energy** – No more relying on foreign oil.

✅ **Electric Vehicle Expansion** – We **invest in U.S.-made EVs** and **build nationwide charging stations.**

✅ **Tax Incentives for Home Solar & Wind** – If you install **solar panels or wind energy at home,** you get a **big tax credit.**

✅ **Transition Assistance for Oil & Gas Workers** – If we're moving toward **clean energy,** oil and gas workers **get guaranteed job training in renewables.**

📌 **Clean energy = lower costs, more jobs, and American independence.**

🛡️ Step 5: Smart Defense & Global Leadership

The **U.S. military budget is bigger than the next 10 countries combined** — but that doesn't mean **we're spending wisely.**

🔷 How We Fix It in Year 2:

✅ **Cut Wasteful Military Spending** – No more **billions wasted on outdated weapons programs**.

✅ **Cybersecurity & AI Warfare Investment** – Wars **aren't just fought with tanks anymore** — we invest in **AI, cyber defense, and digital security.**

✅ **Foreign Policy That Makes Sense** – We focus on **economic strength** and **diplomatic leadership,** not **endless wars.**

📌 We stay strong, but we spend smart.

🔄 Recap: What We Accomplish in Year 2

📌 We rebuild infrastructure and create millions of jobs.

📌 We make AI work for workers, not against them.

📌 We make housing affordable again.

📌 **We secure energy independence with clean, American-made power.**

📌 **We strengthen national defense without wasteful spending.**

This is how we expand America's economy for everyone.

📖 CHAPTER 6: YEAR 3 – FINANCIAL FREEDOM & SUSTAINABILITY

We Built It. Now Let's Secure It.

By Year 3, the economy is booming, wages are up, and jobs are plentiful. But if we stop here, we'll **just end up repeating history.**

We've seen this before—**a strong economy that only benefits the top 1%.** We're not doing that again.

This is the year we lock in long-term financial security for ALL Americans.

Here's how we make sure **wealth isn't just created—it's shared fairly.**

💰 Step 1: Middle-Class Tax Relief – "Fair, Not Free Rides"

Let's be real: **Billionaires have been getting away with tax evasion for decades.**

- **Amazon paid $0 in federal taxes** in some years.
- **CEOs have private islands while regular people can't afford rent.**
- **The ultra-rich use loopholes to dodge taxes while workers see their paychecks shrink.**

Enough.

🔷 **The Fix:**

✅ **Lower Taxes for the Middle Class** – If you make under $100K, **you see a tax cut.**

✅ **Ultra-Wealth Tax (But Smartly Done)** – If you're making **over $50 million a year**, you contribute a little more — **not to punish success, but to stop hoarding.**

✅ **Luxury Tax on Mega Purchases** – You want a **$300 million yacht?** Cool. **1% of that goes toward education and healthcare.**

📌 **The working class gets real relief, while the ultra-rich pay their fair share.**

🎓 Step 2: Debt-Free Education & Vocational Training

Not everyone needs a college degree. But everyone deserves a **fair shot at success.**

Right now:

- **College is insanely expensive.**
- **Trade schools & apprenticeships aren't respected like universities.**
- **Student debt is a trillion-dollar crisis.**

We fix that.

🔷 **The Plan:**

✅ **Debt-Free Community College** – If your family makes under $100K, your **first two years of college are free.**

✅ **National Apprenticeship & Trade Program** – We **fund and expand vocational schools** so that **electricians, welders, and tech workers** get the same respect (and pay) as college grads.

✅ **AI-Powered Learning Hubs in Minority Communities** – We use **AI to customize learning programs** for students in **underserved areas** so they **aren't left behind.**

✅ **Student Loan Reform** – No more **interest rates higher than your mortgage.** We **refinance federal loans at 1-2% interest**, so people can actually **pay them off.**

📌 **Education should be a stepping stone, not a financial trap.**

💼 Step 3: Closing the Racial Wealth Gap

The wealth gap didn't happen by accident.

For generations, Black, Latino, and Indigenous communities were **systematically locked out** of wealth-building opportunities.

- **Redlining kept Black families from buying homes.**
- **Banks charged minorities higher interest rates.**
- **Corporations paid Black and Brown workers less for the same jobs.**

That stops now.

🔷 **The Plan:**

✅ **Equal Pay Enforcement** – AI audits ensure **no company can underpay women or minorities.**

✅ **First-Time Minority Homebuyer Grants** – We expand **home loan access** for historically excluded communities.

✅ **Black & Latino Entrepreneurship Fund** – Direct **federal investment** in minority-owned businesses—**because Wall Street has gotten enough handouts.**

📌 **We're not asking for handouts—we're demanding an even playing field.**

🏠 Step 4: Wealth-Building for Everyone, Not Just the Rich

We've been told for decades that **"if you work hard, you'll get ahead."**

That sounds nice, but here's the truth: **You need access to wealth-building tools, or you'll stay stuck.**

🔷 **How We Fix It:**

✅ **Affordable Housing Expansion** – We build **millions of affordable, high-quality homes** so that homeownership **isn't just for the rich.**

✅ **Retirement Security for All** – We create a **universal retirement savings plan** that every worker **has access to, even gig workers.**

✅ **AI-Driven Investment Tools for Everyone** – The rich use **AI-powered stock trading** to build wealth—**so should everyone else.** We create **free AI investing tools** for regular people.

📌 **You shouldn't have to be rich to have financial security.**

🛡️ **Step 5: Economic Security = National Security**

If we really want to **keep America strong**, it's **not just about military spending.**

A strong country means:

- **People aren't drowning in debt.**
- **Families can afford to live.**
- **Everyone has a shot at financial freedom.**

🔷 **How We Secure the Future:**

✅ **Protect Workers from AI Takeover** – If AI replaces jobs, companies

pay into retraining programs.

✅ **Make Corporations Pay Taxes (For Real This Time)** – No more tax

havens, no more loopholes.

✅ **Rebuild Trust in Government** – When people **see their lives**

improving, trust is restored.

📌 **A strong economy = a strong nation.**

🔄 Recap: What We Accomplish in Year 3

📌 **We cut taxes for the middle class, not the rich.**

📌 **We make college & trade schools affordable.**

📌 **We close the racial wealth gap and expand homeownership.**

📌 **We create long-term financial security for every American.**

This is how we create lasting prosperity.

📖 CHAPTER 7: YEAR 4 – AMERICA'S GLOBAL COMEBACK

America Should Be Leading—So Let's Lead

For too long, we've been **falling behind** while other countries **race ahead.**

- China dominates manufacturing.
- Europe is ahead in green energy.
- The U.S. used to be the leader in tech and space—now billionaires are doing the government's job.

It's time to **take our leadership back**—but do it the **right way.**

- Not through bullying other nations.
- But by leading in technology, economy, and diplomacy.

Here's how we **make America the global leader of the future.**

🌍 Step 1: "Made in America" Trade Deals – Bring Jobs Home

The old way of trade? **Letting corporations outsource jobs while working Americans suffer.**

The new way? **We make trade deals that actually benefit American workers.**

🔷 **The Plan:**

✅ **No More Free Rides for Outsourcing** – If a U.S. company moves jobs overseas, **they lose tax breaks.**

✅ **Tax Incentives for Companies That Manufacture in America** – If you keep **factories, call centers, and**

production in the U.S., you get a tax break.

✅ **Fair Trade, Not Fake Free Trade** – We negotiate **deals that protect American workers** instead of just maximizing corporate profits.

📌 **We don't shut down global trade—we make it fair.**

🚀 Step 2: Leading in AI, Space, and Technology

Right now, **the biggest breakthroughs in AI, robotics, and space exploration** are being made by **private billionaires instead of the U.S. government.**

That's **dangerous**—because if we don't lead in these fields, **other countries will.**

🔷 **The Plan:**

✅ **Massive Investment in AI & Tech Research** – The U.S. government should be **funding the next generation of AI, robotics, and cybersecurity**, not just private corporations.

✅ **Reclaim NASA's Leadership in Space** – No more letting **billionaires control space exploration—NASA leads, private companies assist.**

✅ **AI Ethics & Global Standards** – We **set the rules** for AI development **before China and Big Tech do.**

📌 **If we lead in AI, space, and tech, we lead the future.**

🌱 Step 3: Climate Leadership That Makes Economic Sense

Some people still act like **we have to choose between saving the planet and growing the economy.**

That's **nonsense.**

🔷 **The Plan:**

✅ **Lead the Global Clean Energy Market** – The U.S. should be the **#1 producer of solar panels, wind turbines, and electric cars**—not China.

✅ **Incentivize Green Jobs & Innovation** – We invest in **clean energy jobs, not just oil & gas.**

✅ **Cut Pollution Without Killing Industry** – AI-powered **climate**

tracking helps **companies reduce emissions efficiently,** instead of just slapping them with fines.

📌 **Fighting climate change isn't just good for the planet—it's good for business.**

🤝🤝 **Step 4: Smart Diplomacy & Strong Alliances**

For years, the U.S. has been stuck in a **cycle of wars, bad trade deals, and weak foreign policy.**

🔷 **The Plan:**

✅ **Smart Power, Not Just Military Power** – Strengthen **alliances, trade, and diplomacy** so we **don't have to fight endless wars.**

✅ **Strengthen NATO & Global Partnerships** – Instead of being the **world's policeman,** we become **the world's problem solver.**

✅ **Use Economic Strength as Leverage** – The U.S. should be **the #1 economic force in the world**—not just the **biggest spender on military.**

📌 **America wins through leadership, not just brute force.**

🔄 **Recap: What We Accomplish in Year 4**

📌 We bring jobs back to America with smart trade deals.

📌 We lead in AI, space, and technology—because the future belongs to the innovators.

📌 We make climate leadership an economic advantage.

📌 We use smart diplomacy instead of endless wars.

This is how we position America as the leader of the 21st century.

🏆 The End of Our First Term – What We've Built

After **four years**, here's what we've accomplished:

✅ A government that actually works.

✅ A strong, fair economy where workers thrive.

✅ A justice system that serves everyone, not just the rich.

✅ AI-powered efficiency, transparency, and innovation.

✅ Global leadership that benefits American workers.

And most importantly? **People trust their government again—because it finally works for them.**

📖 CHAPTER 8: THE FUTURE OF LEADERSHIP & AI

What Happens Next?

We did it.

We **rebuilt trust, fixed the economy, created millions of jobs, made government work for the people, and positioned America as a global leader.**

But here's the thing: **Progress is only as strong as the people who protect it.**

- **A great system can be dismantled if the wrong people take over.**
- **A fair economy can be reversed if greed takes control again.**
- **AI can either be a tool for equality—or a tool for oppression.**

So the **real challenge** isn't just **winning once**—it's **making sure we never have to start from scratch again.**

This chapter is about **how we secure progress for the long haul.**

🚀 Step 1: Future-Proofing Leadership

Leadership in the **AI era** isn't about being the loudest voice in the room—it's about being **the smartest, fairest, and most adaptable.**

🔷 **How We Train the Next Generation of Leaders:**

✅ **AI-Powered Decision-Making** – Future leaders should **use AI to make data-driven policies, not just political promises.**

✅ **No More Career Politicians** – Leadership shouldn't be about **staying in power—it should be about serving the people.** We push for **term limits and fresh perspectives.**

✅ **Ethics & Accountability in Leadership** – AI can **track campaign promises, voting records, and corruption risks**—so no leader can get away with lying.

📌 **Leadership evolves. The old way is done.**

🤖 Step 2: AI as a Tool—Not a Master

The biggest question about AI isn't **"How powerful can it become?"**

It's **"Who controls it?"**

🔷 **How We Ensure AI is Used for Good:**

✅ **AI Transparency Laws** – AI systems **must be open, explainable, and accountable.** No secret algorithms deciding who gets hired, fired, or policed.

✅ **AI for the People, Not Just Corporations** – AI **shouldn't just make billionaires richer—it should be used to eliminate bias, streamline government, and improve lives.**

✅ **Preventing AI from Replacing Leadership** – AI **advises, but humans decide.** Leaders **must remain accountable** for policies, no matter how advanced AI becomes.

📌 **AI should serve people, not control them.**

🌍 Step 3: Global Collaboration & Ethical Tech Development

The U.S. isn't the **only** country using AI.

- **China is racing ahead with AI surveillance.**
- **Europe is setting AI safety standards.**
- **Big Tech companies have more AI power than governments.**

We **can't afford to sit back.**

🔷 **The Plan for Ethical AI on a Global Scale:**

✅ **Global AI & Cybersecurity Treaties** – We **work with allies** to create rules that **protect privacy, security, and fairness.**

✅ **Ban AI-Powered Mass Surveillance** – No government should use AI to

oppress citizens. We fight for **AI ethics worldwide.**

✅ **America as the Global AI Leader** – The U.S. leads **AI research, development, and ethical standards** to **ensure AI benefits humanity, not just corporations.**

📌 **AI isn't just a tech issue—it's a human rights issue.**

🛡️ Step 4: Guarding Against Corruption & Greed

Power always tries to creep back into the hands of the few.

If we don't build **permanent protections**, we'll just end up **back where we started.**

🔷 **How We Lock in Progress:**

✅ **AI-Powered Government Watchdog** – A **real-time system that detects fraud, waste, and corruption** in government spending.

✅ **Citizen Oversight Boards** – Everyday people should have

a **direct say in how AI is used in government and business.**

✅ **Laws Against Corporate & Political AI Manipulation** – No AI should be used to **spread misinformation or rig elections.**

📌 **We've seen what unchecked power can do. We're not letting it happen again.**

🔄 Final Recap: The Future is Ours to Shape

📌 **Leadership evolves—we train future leaders to use AI responsibly.**

📌 **AI serves the people, not corporations or governments.**

📌 **The U.S. leads in ethical AI development and global collaboration.**

📌 **We build permanent safeguards against corruption and greed.**

This isn't just about one presidency—it's about setting up the future for generations to come.

🎤 Final Message: The Legacy We Leave Behind

We started with **a broken system**—and we rebuilt it.

We created a **fair economy, a functional government, and a nation that leads the world in AI, innovation, and justice.**

But this book **isn't just about what we did.**

It's about what **YOU** can do.

- **If you're a voter—demand better leadership.**
- **If you're a leader—govern with truth and fairness.**
- **If you're a business owner—use AI for innovation, not exploitation.**
- **If you're part of the next generation—don't wait for change. Make it happen.**

Because at the end of the day, **this isn't just about politics.**

It's about **building a future where leadership actually works—for all of us.**

📖 EPILOGUE: THE FUTURE IS OURS TO CREATE

The work isn't done.

Yes, we've laid out **a roadmap for smarter leadership, economic fairness, and AI-driven governance that actually works.**

Yes, we've **rebuilt trust, secured prosperity, and positioned America as a leader in the future.**

But **progress isn't a finish line.**

- **It's a relay race.**
- **Each generation takes the baton and runs as far as they can.**
- **Then they pass it on.**

Now, it's **your turn.**

📌 **If you're a voter — demand better leadership.**

📌 **If you're an entrepreneur — build businesses that uplift people, not just profits.**

📌 **If you're in politics — lead with truth, innovation, and fairness.**

📌 **If you're part of the next generation — use technology, creativity, and activism to push progress further.**

The future **isn't something we wait for.**

It's something we create.

So let's get to work.

📖 ACKNOWLEDGMENTS

This book wouldn't be possible without the people who **shaped my thinking, supported my vision, and inspired me to push forward—even when the system told me to stay in my lane.**

First and foremost, **I want to thank myself**—yes, **ME**—for having the courage, the resilience, and the vision to create something powerful. If I didn't believe in myself, this book wouldn't exist.

To **all the voices who have been silenced, overlooked, or ignored**—this book is for you.

To **my family and friends** who have supported me through every step of my journey—your love and belief in me kept me going.

To **the leaders, activists, and change-makers throughout history** who fought to level the playing field—your work paved the way for what we're building now.

To **every reader who picked up this book**—thank you. You are part of this movement now. You are part of the future.

And finally — to AI.

(*Yeah, I said it.*)

Because without the rapid advancement of AI, **this book might not have existed.** But the real lesson isn't that AI wrote it — it's that AI helped **me** bring this vision to life.

That's the future we're fighting for: **One where technology and humanity work together — not against each other.**

This is just the beginning.

Contact Information:

Lakisha Monique Swift
P.O. Box 492
Los Angeles, CA 90078-0492

ISBN:

ISBN 978-1-967688-01-2 (Paperback)

ABOUT THE AUTHOR

Lakisha Monique Swift is a **visionary, leader, and truth-teller** who believes that **government should actually work for the people**—not just corporations, lobbyists, and the ultra-wealthy. With a background in **business, entertainment, HR, and activism**, she's seen firsthand how **power, money, and leadership** shape the world.

A firm believer in **common sense over nonsense**, Lakisha brings a **bold, witty, and no-BS** approach to politics, leadership, and the role of AI in the future of governance. She knows that **real change** isn't just about talking—it's about **doing the work** and creating a system where **everyone has a fair shot at success.**

When she's not writing, speaking, or strategizing world domination (*the good kind, don't worry*), she's living life unapologetically—**breaking barriers, pushing boundaries, and making sure her voice (and the voices of others) are heard.**

This book is just the beginning. **The movement starts now.**

📌 NOW IT'S YOUR TURN: THINK, REFLECT, AND SHAPE THE FUTURE

(A Personal Reflection Section at the End of the Book, with Original Lakisha Monique Swift Quotes)

Alright, **you made it through** this book—**now what?** You read my thoughts, my vision, and my plan. But this isn't just about **what I think**—this is about **what YOU believe, too.**

Because let's be real—**four years from now, things could be wildly different.** When you come back and read what you wrote today, will you still feel the same way? Will the world have changed for the better? Will YOU have changed?

This is your moment to **document your thoughts in real time.** So **before you start writing**, take a second and write down today's **date and time**. One day, when you look back, you might just have a **WOW moment.**

📌 Make It Personal: Your Own Story Starts Here

(Because this book isn't just about what I think—it's about YOU.)

Before you dive into these reflection questions, take a moment to **make this book yours.** Think of it as your own personal **time capsule**—something you might look back on years from now and say, *"Wow, I really thought this way back then?"* Or maybe you'll say, *"Damn, I was onto something!"*

Either way, let's **lock in this moment.**

📌 **Write Your Personal Details Below:**

📝 **Your Name:** _____

📍 **Where You Are Right Now:** _____

📅 **Today's Date:** _____

⏳ **Time:** _____

🎯 **One Thing You Believe to Be True About the Future:**
(Example: "AI will take over everything" or "The economy will be even worse" or "We'll finally get things right")

_____

_____

_____

_____

_____

_____

🌍 **One Change You Hope to See in the World:**
(Example: "Equal pay for all" or "A government that actually listens" or "More Black and Brown people in power")

_____

💡 A Message to Your Future Self:

(What do you want to remind yourself when you come back and read this later?)

🔥 **Now that you've made this book yours, let's get into it! Your voice matters.** Your future self is waiting to see what you thought today — so don't hold back!

🚀 **Turn the page, and let's go.**

📌 Chapter 1: Why Government is Broken (And How We Fix It)

📅 **Date:** _____ 🕐 **Time:** _____

💬 **Lakisha Monique Swift Quote:**
"A broken system doesn't fix itself. Either you change the rules, or you play to win and rewrite them." – Lakisha Swift

💭 **Reflection Question:**
*If you woke up tomorrow and I handed you the keys to the White House, what's the FIRST thing you'd fix? Be real—what's actually **doable** and not just a nice idea?*

📖 **Revisit Chapter 1** to see where the government keeps screwing up—and where we can start fixing it.

✍️✍️✍️ ✍️✍️✍️Your vision for the future:

_____

_____

_____

_____

_____

_____

📌 Chapter 2: A Balanced Economy – Thriving Capitalism with Fair Play

📅 **Date:** _____ 🕐 **Time:** _____

💬 **Lakisha Monique Swift Quote:**

"Money doesn't trickle down, it gets hoarded at the top. If we want a fair economy, we have to stop treating billionaires like an endangered species." – Lakisha Swift

💭 **Reflection Question:**

Be honest—do you think the economy is designed for everyone to succeed, or is it rigged? Should the rich pay more, or should we all just work harder?

📖 **Revisit Chapter 2** to see how we can **build an economy that actually works for everyone**.

✍️✍️✍️ ✍️✍️✍️Your vision for the future:

_____

_____

_____

_____

_____

_____

📌 Chapter 3: The Role of AI in Modern Governance

📅 **Date:** _____ 🕐 **Time:** _____

💬 **Lakisha Monique Swift Quote:**
"Technology is only as dangerous as the people programming it. If we don't teach AI our values, it will only reflect our worst mistakes." – Lakisha Swift

💭 **Reflection Question:**
Would you trust an AI-powered president? No scandals, no corruption—just cold, hard logic. Or does that sound like a disaster waiting to happen?

📖 **Revisit Chapter 3** to explore **how AI could reshape government.**

✍️✍️✍️ ✍️✍️✍️Your vision for the future:

_____

_____

_____

_____

_____

_____

📌 Chapter 4: Year 1 – Stabilization & Trust-Building

📅 **Date:** _____ 🕐 **Time:** _____

💬 **Lakisha Monique Swift Quote:**

"Trust in leadership isn't given—it's earned. And some of these folks out here are overdrafted in credibility." – Lakisha Swift

💭 **Reflection Question:**

What would it take for YOU to trust leadership again? Transparency? Better policies? A brand-new system? What would actually make you believe in the government?

📖 **Revisit Chapter 4** to see how we **rebuild trust in Year 1**.

👏👏👏 👏👏 Your vision for the future:

_____

_____

_____

_____

_____

_____

📌 Chapter 5: Year 2 – Growth & Expansion

📅 **Date:** _____   🕐 **Time:** _____

💬 **Lakisha Monique Swift Quote:**
"If you can't afford to pay your workers a living wage, you don't have a business—you have a hustle." – Lakisha Swift

💭 **Reflection Question:**
If you could rewrite the rules for jobs and business, what would you change? Should companies be forced to pay higher wages, or should people just learn better skills?

📖 **Revisit Chapter 5** to see how **we fix the job market** and **balance fair capitalism**.

✊✊✊ ✊✊✊ Your vision for the future:

_____

_____

_____

_____

_____

_____

📌 Chapter 6: Year 3 – Financial Freedom & Sustainability

📅 **Date:** _____ 🕐 **Time:** _____

💬 **Lakisha Monique Swift Quote:**
"We can't keep acting like wealth is only for the lucky few. If financial freedom isn't an option for everybody, then the system is by design, not accident." – Lakisha Swift

💭 **Reflection Question:**
If the government gave every citizen a basic monthly income, would people thrive—or get lazy? Would it help struggling families, or would people take advantage of it?

📖 **Revisit Chapter 6** to see how we **secure financial freedom for all.**

✍️ ✍️ ✍️ ✍️ ✍️ ✍️ Your vision for the future:

_____

_____

_____

_____

_____

_____

📌 Chapter 7: Year 4 – America's Global Comeback

📅 **Date:** _____ 🕐 **Time:** _____

💬 **Lakisha Monique Swift Quote:**
"America has two choices: lead the world into the future or fall behind and blame everyone else." – Lakisha Swift

💭 **Reflection Question:**
Should America focus on fixing itself first, or do we have a responsibility to lead the world? Are we helping, or just interfering in global issues?

📖 **Revisit Chapter 7** to explore **America's role as a world leader.**

✍️✍️✍️ ✍️✍️✍️Your vision for the future:

_____

_____

_____

_____

_____

_____

📌 Chapter 8: The Future of Leadership & AI

📅 Date: _____ **🕐 Time:** _____

💬 Lakisha Monique Swift Quote:
"Leadership isn't about controlling people; it's about inspiring them to see a world they can help create." – Lakisha Swift

💭 Reflection Question:
When you think about the future of leadership, do you believe it will be led by human vision or AI logic? Will we keep making the same mistakes, or will we finally find a way to work together—AI, humanity, and all the voices in between?

📖 **Revisit Chapter 8** for insights on **where leadership and AI are headed.**

✍️✍️✍️✍️✍️✍️Your vision for the future:

_____

_____

_____

_____

_____

_____

📌 Final Thought: Where Do We Go From Here?

📅 **Date:** _____ 🕐 **Time:** _____

💬 **Lakisha Monique Swift Quote:**
"The future isn't waiting for permission. Either you build it, or someone else will." – Lakisha Swift

Alright. **Now it's just you and the future.**

Four years from now, do you think we'll be in a better place? Or will we be looking at another broken system, still trying to get it right?

If you're reading this months or even years later, go back and see what you wrote. Are you surprised by your answers? Have your views changed?

👏👏👏👏👏 Your vision for the future:

_____

_____

_____

_____

_____

_____

www.ingramcontent.com/pod-product-compliance
Lightning Source LLC
Chambersburg PA
CBHW041217270326
41931CB00001B/15